THE EXCELLENCY OF CHRIST

John Owen

Vintage Puritan Series
GLH Publishing
LOUISVILLE, KY

Sourced from *The Works of John Owen*. Vol. XII.
Edited by William Goold.

ISBN:
Paperback 978-1-948648-23-3

Contents

Sermon I. 1

Sermon II. 14

Sermon III. 23

Sermon IV. 36

Sermon I.[1]

To the chief Musician upon Shoshannim, for the sons of Korah, Maschil, A Song of loves.
"My heart is inditing a good matter: I speak of the things which I have made touching the King; my tongue is the pen of a ready writer," etc.
Psalm xlv. 1-3.

The whole Book of Psalms hath a peculiar respect unto Jesus Christ, either directly or in the person of David, who was his greatest personal type, next to Aaron and Melchizedeck; but there are some psalms that are altogether *directly* prophetical of him and of his offices, namely, the 2nd psalm is prophetical of his kingdom; the 16th psalm, of the work of his mediation and obedience to God therein; the 22nd, of his priestly office, his sufferings, death, his resurrection, and intercession; the 40th, of his oblation and suffering; the 72nd, of his kingly and prophetical power and glorious regard unto his people; the 68th, of his glorious exaltation; and this 45th psalm is a prophecy and description of his person, and his kingly office, and of the espousals of him and his church.

The title of the psalm is, "To the chief Musician upon Shoshannim, for the sons of Korah, Maschil, A Song of loves."

"To the chief musician;" so למנצח is generally rendered, "To him that excels." As נצח signifies eternal, I have sometimes thought it might be as well rendered, "*In perpetuam rei memoriam;*" — "For an everlasting remembrance." But we may take

---

1 This sermon was preached June 7, 1674, at Stadham.

it in the common acceptation, that it was recommended unto him that did preside over the rest of the Levites in the worship of God in the temple, by singing on instruments of music.

"Upon Shoshannim." The word signifies lilies; whether it was a musical *instrument* or a certain *tune*, we know not, neither do the Jews.

"For the sons of Korah." Who these were we may see, 1 Chron. ix. 19, "The Korahites were over the work of the service, keepers of the gates of the tabernacle," etc. What were they else? Verse 33, "These are the singers, chief of the fathers of the Levites, who remaining in the chambers were free;" for they were employed in the work of singing the praises of God with instruments of music day and night.

David was the first who brought musical instruments into the solemn worship of God; not but that they did occasionally make use of timbrels and cymbals in the praises of God before, but he was the first that brought in a great number of musical instruments into the worship of God. And he speaks expressly, in 1 Chron. xxiii. 5, of praising God with instruments of music, "which," says he, "I made." He did it by the direction of the Spirit of God; otherwise he ought not to have done it: for so it is said, 1 Chron. xxviii. 12, when he had established all the ordinances of the temple, — *the pattern of all that he had by the Spirit*. And verse 19, "All this, said David, the Lord made me understand in writing by his hand upon me, even all the works of this pattern." It was all revealed unto him by the Holy Spirit, without which he could have introduced nothing at all into the worship of God. The Lord prepared him for this service while he was a shepherd; at which time he had attained great skill in singing on musical instruments.

And I cannot but observe, by the way, that it is

a great mercy when God will engage the natural faculties and abilities of men, especially wherein they are excellent, in any way of his service. David had got an excellency in this faculty, and God engages it in his service. And those that had skill therein, and were not so engaged, are condemned in the prophet Amos, chap. vi. 5. What were they condemned for? Why, that they would invent *instruments of music like David.* David did it to serve the Lord; and they did it to serve their lusts. Where men have any peculiar faculty or ability, it is an unspeakable mercy to have it engaged for God; for otherwise it will certainly be engaged for the devil: and, to render the mercy more singular, I think it is evident the devil hath got the use and advantage of natural faculties and abilities above what is given up to God.

Again: this was David's special inclination; whence he is called "The sweet psalmist of Israel." The edge of his spirit lay to it. And we may observe, that it is an excellent mercy when the edge of our spirits, in special inclination, is engaged for the service of God. Prov. xxvii. 17, as "iron sharpeneth iron; so a man sharpeneth the countenance of his friend." Every man hath an edge; and there are several ways whereby it is sharpened. There is no man but *cuts* one way or other; and company and society is the great means whereby the edge is sharpened. One cuts to the world, another to pleasures, to lusts; and such company makes him more sharp. It is well when the edge of a man's spirit is set for the things of God, and he has some to sharpen that edge; for that way that a man's edge is set, *that way is he.* He may do something in the worship of God; but if his edge be to the world, that way is he; and if his edge be to lust and pleasure, that way is he. Now, here was David; the special inclination and edge of his spirit was set towards God, and so was employed of God.

There is a general title given to this psalm, "Maschil;" that is, song to make wise, or to give instruction. They are the things of Christ that, in an especial manner, are suited to give instruction to the church of God.

The special matter of the psalm is, "A Song of loves." And why is it called "loves"? It may be upon three accounts: 1. Because the psalm mentions a *mutual* and *interchangeable* love. It is not only of the love of Christ to his church, nor only of the love of the church unto Christ, but it is mutual, of the love of Christ to the church, and of the church to Christ; so that it is a song of loves. 2. It may be put in the plural number by way of *eminency*, which is frequent in the Hebrew; "of loves,"—that is, of *the most excellent love*, such as none other is to be compared unto it. 3. It may be called so, cause of the *manifold fruits* of that one single love that is between Christ and his church. Though it be but a single love on each hand, yet various are the fruits of it; which will be described in the next verse.

I principally look upon it to be called so in the second sense, cause it is more eminent than any other love in the world; the mystical, spiritual love that is between Christ and the church, is the most excellent love.

It is "A Song of loves" I shall not speak unto you of the nature of *songs*. "Let him that is merry," saith James, chap. v. 13 (or in a rejoicing, cheerful frame of heart and spirit), "sing psalms:" so that singing was a means appointed of God whereby men should express their joy in a way of thankfulness.

Thus this title of the psalm will yield us these two observations: I. That the espousals of Christ and his church, or the *mutual love* that is between Christ and his church, is *a subject-matter for a song of great joy.* II. It is not a song of love, but it is a song of *loves.* I observe from thence, that there is no love like the love of Christ to his church in the day of espousals, and to every believing soul; it hath an eminency in it above all other love whatever.

I. This love of Christ and the church in their espousals is matter of great joy and rejoicing:

1. It is so *to God himself.* He expresses the frame of his heart therein, Zeph. iii. 17, "He will rejoice over thee with joy; he will rest in his love, he will joy over thee with singing." The union of Christ and a believer (for it is spoken of there), is a matter of unspeakable joy to God himself. Not that God is subject to the like affections with us; but he expresses it to the height in Jer. xxxii. 41, that we may know how the heart of God approves it, "I will rejoice over them to do them good, with my whole heart and with my whole soul:" so that it is a song of loves to God himself. Also in Isa. lxii. 4, 5, "The Lord delighteth in thee, and thy land shall be married. For as a young man marrieth a virgin, so shall thy sons marry thee: and as the bridegroom rejoiceth over the bride, so shall thy God rejoice over thee." Many other places might be given to this purpose.

2. It is matter of joy *to Jesus Christ.* Cant. iii. 11, "Go forth, O ye daughters of Zion, and behold king Solomon with the crown wherewith his mother crowned him in the day of his espousals, and in the day of the gladness of his heart." This Solomon was a type of Christ; and the mother of Christ, that brought forth Christ as to his human nature, was the church: and in the espousals of the church to Christ set a crown upon his head; see Ps. xvi. 6, "The lines," saith Christ, in reference to his church, "are fallen unto me in pleasant places; yea, I have a goodly heritage;"—it is the approbation that Christ gives of his church when

he is espoused unto it, in the day of the gladness of his heart.

3. It is matter of joy to *believers themselves*, 1 Pet. i. 8, "In whom, though now ye see him not, yet believing, ye rejoice with joy unspeakable, and full of glory." It is, I say, matter of joy and praise unto them.

Why are the loves of Christ and his church, or the espousals of Christ and a believing soul, matter of such joy as to be the subject of a song of loves to God himself, to Jesus Christ, and to believers?

(1.) Because, on the part of God, it is that wherein the glorious design and *purpose* of his grace is *accomplished*, and his goodness satisfied. God doth all things for "the praise of the glory of his grace," Eph. i. 6. Wherefore, when this grace of God is accomplished, and his goodness satisfied, it is matter of rejoicing unto God. When he had laid the foundation of *the old creation*, and all the sons of God shouted for joy, God himself looked upon all, and, "behold, it was very good;" he approved his whole work: and when he carried on the work of the *new creation*, whereof this I am speaking of is the greatest instance, even the espousal loves between Christ and a believing soul, having accomplished such a work of grace, and power, and goodness as this is, God himself doth approve of it; it is matter of joy unto him.

(2.) It is matter of joy to Jesus Christ, because "he sees of the travail of his soul, and is satisfied." This is that he laboured for, Isa. liii. 11, etc. It was matter of joy to Jacob, when he had obtained Rachel to be his wife, that he had got that he laboured for: "He served for a wife," saith the Holy Ghost, Hos. xii. 12. Why, the Lord Jesus Christ, when he hath united his church to himself (and in proportion, any believing soul), he hath that which he hath laboured for, he sees of the travail of his soul. It cost him prayers and tears, blood and death; but now he sees what it is come unto: it hath produced this bride for him, or believing souls to be united to him; and he is satisfied. He fulfilled a hard service; but it was for his bride, in whom his soul delighted, as he does in every believing soul, when he hath made them comely through his comeliness, or in and through the righteousness he puts upon them.

(3.) It is certainly a matter of joy to all believers themselves, because *it instates them in those new relations*, and in that condition, which they, for their part, never ought to have expected or looked for, as to any thing that was in themselves. And therefore the prophet Isaiah, Isa. liv. 5, calls upon the church to rejoice exceedingly, because "thy Maker is thine husband; the Lord of hosts is his name; and thy Redeemer the Holy One of Israel; The God of the whole earth shall he be called." All grace and privilege, all mercy, pardon, every thing else we enjoy in this world, and hope for in another, depends upon this, of relation unto Jesus Christ; therefore, certainly it is a matter of joy and rejoicing to believers.

That which we may learn from hence, by way of *use*, is,

1. The *infinite wisdom*, goodness, and condescension of God, in *disposing the way* of saving poor sinners so as that it shall be matter of joy and rejoicing to him, to Jesus Christ, and to believers themselves. It was infinite wisdom and grace, that God would dispose any way for the salvation of his creatures. He gave out a way to Adam, whereby (by perfect obedience) he might have attained life, immortality, and glory. That was not a way that did issue in such great joy to God, to Christ, or to ourselves, as this doth, where God is glorified, Christ satisfied, and believers themselves are surprised. We were poor, desolate, for-

lorn, lost creatures; and that God should bring us into a way of saving us, so as that the heart of God and Christ, and our own hearts, should rejoice in it;—this calls for our admiration. I know it is hard for us to believe it; yet I know it is true, that God himself is rejoiced, and Christ rejoices in the taking of any one soul into espousals with himself. And, which may add more, all the angels in heaven rejoice too, Luke xv. 10, "There is joy in the presence of the angels of God over one sinner that repenteth;" because God is so glorified, and Christ so exalted. God hath put this way of converting and saving sinners into such a channel as will tend to his glory, and the glory of Christ, and so be matter of joy unto them.

2. Let us inquire whether we have found, or do find, this joy *in our own hearts*. Is the remembrance of the closing of our hearts with Christ a song of loves unto us? Truly, if our loves be earnest and intent upon *other* things, we find joy and refreshment *in them*; but are we not dead and cold to the thoughts of this great and excellent advantage, of being *espoused to Christ*, as all believers are? If so, it is but a sad evidence we are truly so espoused. Alas! if a poor beggar, a deformed creature, should be taken into the espousals of a great prince, would she not be sensible of it? We are poor, deformed, woeful, sinful, polluted creatures; and for us to be taken into this relation with Jesus Christ!—*where are our hearts*? Why do not we rejoice in the Lord with joy unspeakable, and full of glory? Is it not because Christ hath not our whole hearts? because we are not so entirely with him and for him in our affections as becomes this relation? because the world hath too much hold upon us? Shall God rejoice, and Christ rejoice, shall it be a song of loves to God and Christ that we are brought into this relation, and these dull hearts of ours be no farther affected with it? We

ought to be ashamed to think how little we are concerned in this so great a privilege, how little lifted up above the world, and alienated from the world; if, indeed, we are partakers of this mercy.

II. The second observation from its being a song of loves, is this, that there is *no love like* to the love between Christ and the souls of believers. There are flaming loves in some to their lusts, in others to the world, that even devour them; but yet I will say again, upon ten thousand accounts, there is no love like to the love between Christ and the souls of believers.

Should we go to speak now of the love of Christ, on the one side, it is an ocean, we cannot fathom it. The best act of our souls towards Christ's love is *admiration*, astonishing admiration, till the heart is quite overwhelmed with it, till our thoughts and understandings are, as it were, lost; the soul is taken out of itself, and laid in the dust as nothing, to be swallowed up in a holy contemplation of the unspeakable, inconceivable love of Jesus Christ.

I will name three heads of it, that may help us, in this admiration, to see that it is a love that is *inimitable*: the fiery loves of men, after this world and their lusts, are not to be named the same day with it:

1. Consider it in its *condescension*. Now, I think we shall all confess that this love is inimitable, because nothing but infinite, divine power and wisdom could work such an effect as was the condescension of the Son of God, out of his love to take our nature upon him, to become flesh as we are; and God never wrought it, nor will, *but in that instance*, to all eternity: and therefore, this love hath the pre-eminence above all other loves whatsoever. In Phil. ii. 6–8, it is there set forth, where he unites those things that are set at an infinite distance of being. He stoops so low, that he saith,

Ps. xxii. 6, "I am a worm, and no man;" he comes to the lowest condition mankind can be reduced unto in this condescension: and surely this hath a pre-eminence above all other loves whatsoever.

2. The love of Christ was manifested *in his suffering* in that condition. You know what he suffered, and what he suffered for. He suffered to bear *the guilt* of our sins, so to take away the wrath of God; he suffered to wash away the filth of our sins, so to take away shame and confusion from our souls; he suffered to redeem us from the world, poor captive creatures as we were, that we might be his own: and therefore, God gives us the type of it in the prophet Hosea, Hos. iii., by a harlot; and Christ bought us when we were harlots with the world (our hearts going after sin and Satan), that we might be his property. He suffered for us, so as to bear the guilt of our iniquities, that there may be no wrath from God upon us. "I will pay," saith Christ, "what I never took away." "For a good man," it is possible, "some would even dare to die," Rom. v. 7; but saith he, "Here is love, Christ died for us when we were sinners, when we were enemies." "He loved us, and washed us in his own blood," that we may be purified from the filth of our sins; he loved us, and redeemed us out of every kindred and nation in the world. Here lay all misery;—the guilt of sin, that rendered us obnoxious to the curse of God; and the filth of sin, that made us odious to God, and kept us under the power of the world. This love hath suffered on purpose to redeem us from all this.

3. The care and *tenderness which the Lord Jesus Christ continues* to manifest towards us, now he is in heaven, while we are upon the earth, is *another fruit of this love*. Heb. v. 2, this high priest knows how to "have compassion on the ignorant, and them that are out of the way." Chap. iv. 15, He

hath been "touched with the feeling of our infirmities," and "in all points tempted like as we;" and "he ever liveth to make intercession for us." In these things he expresses his love to, and care for, his people.

On the other side, I say, the love of believers to Christ is inexpressible, or beyond all other love whatsoever.

1. In a way *of value*. Matt. xiii. 45, when the merchant-man had found the precious pearl, he sells all he hath to buy it. Believers will part with all they have to obtain Christ; for they prefer him above all. What will they not part with, and what *do they not* part with and deny, for Christ? Whereby you may see it is a love that is transcendent to all other loves.

(1.) They part with their sin, lust, and corruption. There is not a believer in the world but hath naturally as great a love of, and adherence to, sin, lust, and corruption, as the highest debauched person upon the face of the earth; but a believer will part with them all, subdue them all, so that he might win Christ: which manifests it to be a transcendent love. And they that will not do this are not believers. If our hearts are not engaged to the mortifying of all sin, lust, and corruption, as he enables us, we are not married to Christ; for "they that are Christ's have crucified the flesh, with the affections and lusts,' " Gal. v. 24.

(2.) They will part with their *righteousness* for Christ. This was that the Jews would not give up, that they might obtain justification. They had a righteousness which was according to the law; and, saith the apostle, Rom. x. 3, "They will not submit to the righteousness of God, but go about to establish their own righteousness." All the righteousness which is in the world, that the men of the world value before Christ, while they are engaged in their lusts and pleasures, they will not part with it for Christ;—yea, even when they are wrought off their lusts and pleasures by conviction to some duties, yet they will not part with their own righteousness for Christ. But believers will part with theirs, and count it all as loss and dung.

If corruption be subdued, and righteousness be given up, what remains? Truly,

(3.) *Self* remains. If a man denies not himself in lawful things, in any thing that will hinder his walking with God and living unto God, which will make him unfaithful in his place or unfruitful, to please God, he is not worthy of him. If he cannot deny his ease, liberty, peace, profit, or pleasure, he is not, worthy of Jesus Christ. Now, that love which will carry a man out to deny all ungodliness and lust, to renounce all his own righteousness, to lose all he hath wrought in his own strength, to deny himself upon every instance wherein Christ requires him;—this is a transcendent love, above all other love whatsoever.

2. The love of believers manifests itself also *in suffering for Christ*; and O who can tell what the martyrs endured from love to the Lord Jesus!

So that this psalm, which treats of the espousals of Christ and believers, may well have this title, "A Song of loves;" it being the most excellent love.

Two things, from hence, are incumbent upon us:

First. To labour to *get a sense of this love of Christ* upon our hearts. If we are believers, all this love of Christ, who is "King of kings, and Lord of lords," is fixed upon every one of our souls; and it is our great duty to labour to let in a sense of this love of Christ into them. Out of his abundant love and grace, and for no other reason in the world, he loved us when we were strangers, he reconciled us to himself when we were enemies, and engaged in enmity against him; give him, then, the glory of his sovereign grace with respect to your own souls. And,

Secondly. Let us *examine ourselves* whether we have this transcendent love to Jesus Christ in our hearts. If we have, it will continually keep us up to the mortification of lust and corruption, to the renouncing of all self-righteousness, to the denying ourselves; and it will make us continually ready for all the service and suffering Christ shall call us unto.

Sermon II.[2]

> *"My heart is inditing a good matter: I speak of the things which I have made touching the King; my tongue is the pen of a ready writer. Thou art fairer than the children of men; grace is poured into thy lips: therefore God hath blessed thee for ever. Gird thy sword upon thy thigh, O most Mighty, with thy glory and thy majesty."*
> Psalm xlv. 1-3.

This psalm hath three parts. The title of it is, "A Song of loves," which I have already spoken unto; the preface of it, in the 1st verse; and the song itself, from the 2nd verse to the end.

The 1st verse contains a preface to this song of loves: "My heart is inditing a good matter: I speak of the things which I have made touching the King; my tongue is the pen of a ready writer."

I shall offer a few things from these words:

Observe, in general, that he that lays a good foundation makes a good beginning of what he hath to say. It is from his heart. "My heart," saith he, "is inditing." If things do not begin at the heart, whatsoever we do about spiritual things, they are of no value, of no use. We may perform duties, we may pray, and preach, and hear; but if these things do not spring from the heart (that is, from faith, and love, and delight working in the heart), all is lost. A sacrifice without a heart, a silly dove that has no heart, are things God abhors, Hos. vii. 11.

The heart of the psalmist was in this matter;

---
2 This sermon was preached at Stadham, June 7, 1674.

and if our heart be in it, it will be a duty, in our measure and proportion, good and acceptable with God, as it was with him.

There are in the verse two things: I. The subject-matter treated of in this song of loves. II. The manner of expressing it.

I. The subject treated of: 1. In general, that it is *a good matter*. It is not a song about vain, empty things; much less about wicked and sinful things, as the songs of the world are; neither is it only about things that are true, but have no goodness in them: but, saith he, "My heart is inditing a good matter."

2. What this good matter is, is declared: "I speak of the things which I have made touching the King." "The subject," saith he, "of this song of mine is the King; it is no ordinary person." It was the name whereby they called the Messiah, "Christ the Lord," under the Old Testament, who is, indeed, "The Lord of lords, and King of kings." "I have set my King upon my holy hill of Zion," Ps. ii. 6. He was principally prophesied of as "a prince, a ruler, a captain; being to deliver the people of God." He is the subject of the song. And it is limited to things touching or concerning him; as if he had said, "It is not for me, it is not for any mortal man, to conceive or express all the glories and excellencies of the great King, Jesus Christ; but," saith he, "*something touching*, something concerning him."

The best we can reach or attain unto in this world, is only something touching Christ. We cannot yet behold the King in his glory; we cannot see his *uncreated excellencies* or beauties, nor those unspeakable glories of his person, natures, and works, as we shall one day contemplate and behold.

"I speak," saith he, "of the things I have made;" that is, which I have prepared; I will mention only the things which I have composed concerning Christ.

So that the subject of this song is, in general, "a good matter;" in particular, things touching Christ, and such things as the psalmist, through the inspiration of the Holy Ghost, had composed.

II. There is the *manner* of their delivery, both as to their conception and as to outward expression. Their conception, it was in his heart; as to the outward delivery, it was by his tongue. And there is a peculiarity in both. It is not an ordinary conception of the heart, it is not a common expression of the tongue. If you will look into the margin of your Bibles, you will find that what we have rendered here, "inditing," in the original signifies "boiling" or "bubbling up." The word refers to the bubbling up of water in a fountain or spring. The heart of the psalmist was so full of these things of Christ, things touching the King, that they did naturally overflow, as water rising out of a spring naturally flows into the stream, without any labour or difficulty. It was no hard thing to him to speak of the things of Christ; his heart was full of them. O that it was thus with us! It is promised it shall be so. In John iv. 14, Christ hath promised to give his people his Spirit, that "shall be in them as a well of water springing up into everlasting life."

My tongue, saith he, shall not only express it, but in a peculiar manner; "my tongue is the pen of a ready writer."

"A ready writer,"—one speedy, steady, able to set down any thought or conception whatsoever. When we deal about the things of Christ, there is a peculiar manner required both in the conception of the heart and in the expression of the tongue.

Thus I have given you the sense of the words; and I shall now name some observations from them:

First, That the things which concern Jesus Christ are a *good matter to believers*. They are not only true, so as the mind may assent unto them and never be deceived, but they have that in them which is the object of the soul's delight and valuation, and which the soul of a believer cleaves unto. The truth of it is, here lies the great difference between sincere believers and mere hypocrites: hypocrites assent unto the doctrine of the gospel, things touching the King, *as true*, but they never embrace them *as good*; their hearts and affections do not *cleave* unto them, as finding a real sweetness, excellency, and suitableness unto their wants in them: for no man esteems that to be good which is not *suitable* unto him.

Jesus Christ, and the things of Christ, are a good matter unto believers; for,

1. They are very *excellent in themselves*. Col. i. 18, "He hath in all things the pre-eminence." Whatsoever is good in any kind, it centres in Christ. And what is in him is better than that which was in the state of nature; better than what was in the law; better than what is in self-righteousness; better than life itself: so that, from their own nature, they are good things. Give me leave to say they are good things, because they are God's best things. As to temporal good things, take a king or a potentate;—his best things are peculiar treasures, gold and silver, and precious stones; but the things which concern Christ are the best things of the kingdom of heaven.

The things which concern God's only begotten Son, and which concern all the wisdom, grace, love, and power the holy God will exercise in the greatest work he ever set his hand to; surely they are good things. When the psalmist saith it is "a good matter," his meaning is, it is *the best matter* in the world.

2. They are a good matter to believers, because they have received the Spirit, whereby *they are able to discern the excellency of them*.

As to others, it is said, "He shall grow up as a tender plant, and as a root out of a dry ground: he hath no form nor comeliness; and when we shall see him, there is no beauty that we should desire him," Isa. liii. 2. Can we see no goodness, no excellency in Christ, in the grace of Christ, in his ways, in his people, why he should be desired? Believers can, 1 Cor. ii. 7–10. The Spirit of God discovers to them the excellent things of Christ, whereby they find them to be good; whereas to strangers from Christ they seem absurd and foolish things, and no way to be desired. Men of carnal wisdom, that have attained to the highest pitch of reason and ability in the world, they can see neither form nor comeliness in Christ, or the things of Christ; but when God opens the things of Christ by the Spirit, then they see that there is a goodness and an excellency in them.

By way of use. Seeing the things of Christ are good things in themselves, and believers discern their goodness and their excellency; we may do well, then, to inquire whether the things of Christ are good things to us. Then they are good things to us, when we desire them above all other things whatsoever. Phil. iii. 8, "I count all things but loss for the excellency of the knowledge of Christ Jesus my Lord." He could make use of those things he had; but in comparison, his heart did really esteem them all as loss and dung, when they stood in competition with Christ. And pray let us consider how the psalmist hath here stated it. Saith he, "My heart indites, and my tongue professes." It is easy to profess that the things of Christ are good things, and that we esteem all other things as loss and dung; but do our hearts so esteem them? otherwise we come short of what is here intended by the psalmist. Do our hearts really value the good things of Christ, things concerning the glory of his person, his love to his church, the excellency of his kingdom and his rule? The things here treated of; the glory of his person, "Fairer than the children of men;"—the glory of his kingdom, "In thy majesty ride prosperously;" "thy throne O God, is for ever and ever;"—and his love to his church, "Hearken, O daughter, and consider and incline thine ear, forget also thine own people and thy father's house, so shall the King greatly desire thy beauty." Do we value these things, I say, in our very hearts, so as to esteem all other things as loss and dung, that we could freely forego them? Do we find satisfaction in the things of Christ, with and without all other things? *With* other things? It is the will of God, while he intrusts us with other things, that we should use them to his glory; but is our satisfaction in the good things of Christ so high that we can be satisfied *without* other things? Truly, I hope the Lord will help us, that if we come to lose all things for the good things of Christ (and how soon we may come to such a time we know not), we may do it cheerfully and willingly. This I can say, that the nearer some have been to the losing of all things, even life itself, the better Christ hath been unto them. And I would pray for you, that if God should reserve us for such a time as to deprive us of all other things, this may grow upon our hearts, that the things of Christ are better than ever you apprehended. This will carry us through all our darkness and trouble, to be satisfied with them in the want of other things. And take it for your comfort, though you may tremble now at the parting with a hair of your head, as if it was the garment from your back, yet, if you are sincere believers, when you come to part with all, you will do it cheerfully. Christ will come in and enable you so to do. Examine, therefore, yourselves, whether you do not only give a naked assent to the gospel and the things of Christ, or whether you find a goodness in them, a suitableness and satisfaction in them, that it is "a good matter" unto you.

Secondly, Observe from the words, that it is the duty of believers to be making things concerning Jesus Christ: "Things that I have made touching the King." Now, to be making things concerning Jesus Christ, is *to meditate upon him*, to have firm and fixed meditations upon Christ, and upon the glory of his excellencies: this is it that here is called, "The things I have made," composed, framed in my mind. He did not make pictures of Christ, or frame such and such images of him; but he meditated upon Christ. It is called, "Beholding as in a glass the glory of the Lord," in 2 Cor. iii. 18. What is the glory of the Lord? Why, it is the glory of his person, the glory of his kingdom, the glory of his love. Where are these to be seen? They are all represented in the glass. What glass? The glass of the gospel. The gospel hath a reflection upon it of all these glories of Christ, and makes a representation of them unto us. What is our work and business? Why, it is to behold this glory; that is, to contemplate upon it by faith, to meditate upon it, which is here called making "things touching the King." This is also called "Christ's dwelling in us," Eph. iii. 17; and, "The word of Christ dwelling richly in us," Col. iii. 16;—which is, when the soul abounds in thoughts of Christ. I have had more advantage by private thoughts of Christ than by any thing in this world; and I think when a soul hath satisfying and exalting thoughts of Christ himself, his person and his glory, it is the way whereby Christ dwells in such a soul. If I have observed any thing by experience, it is this, a man may take the measure of his growth and decay in grace according to his thoughts and meditations upon the person of Christ, and the glory of Christ's kingdom, and of his love. A heart that is inclined to converse with Christ as he is represented in the gospel, is a thriving heart; and if estranged from it and backward to it, it is under deadness and decays.

"Touching the King." The psalmist hath respect unto Christ as a king. Hence,

Thirdly, Observe that there is a peculiar glory in the kingly office of Jesus Christ, that we should daily exercise our thoughts about. The comfort, joy, and refreshment of believers, in this world, lie in the kingly power of Christ. What a view is there taken of him in Isa. lxiii. 1, "Who is this that cometh from Edom, with dyed garments from Bozrah? this that is glorious in his apparel, travelling in the greatness of his strength? I that speak in righteousness, mighty to save;" and which refers us to but one part of his kingly office, namely, to the power he will put forth in destroying his enemies. It is generally thought that Edom under the Old Testament shadows forth Rome under the New. This is a glorious description of Christ going forth in the greatness of his power, when the year of his redeemed is come, and the day of vengeance is in his heart. How dreadful will it be to the world! how glorious in the eyes of believers! when we shall see him glorious in his apparel, travelling in the greatness of his strength, till he hath destroyed all his stubborn adversaries.

There is a peculiar glory in the kingdom of Christ, that we ought much, for our relief, to meditate upon. If we could behold the internal and external workings of Christ; what he hath done, what he will do, how that certainly he will save every believer, how that certainly he will destroy every enemy, how infallible in his grace, and never-failing in his vengeance; we should then see a peculiar glory in his kingdom.

Fourthly, Observe, that when a heart is full of love to Christ, it *will run over*; then men will be speaking of Christ, and of his glory. "We believe," saith the apostle, "and therefore speak," 2 Cor. iv. 13. If we do believe, we shall speak. And saith the apostle, Acts iv. 20, when they said, "Speak no more in this name," saith he, "We cannot but speak the things which we have seen and heard;" we *cannot but* speak them. On the contrary, there is sad evidence how little there is of love in the hearts of men towards Christ. Alas! look about to the multitudes of them that are called Christians; when do you hear a word of him? when do you meet with a heart overflowing with love to Christ? Some speak of him to blaspheme him, some to the reproach of him; but for a natural readiness to speak for him, where do we find it? Yet if the heart be filled, it will boil over. There are some that pass for professors; you shall very seldom hear a word of Christ from them. If a man would make himself a reproach in the world, he cannot better do it than by owning Christ and his Spirit before men.

Fifthly, and lastly, That profession alone is acceptable to God, and useful in the church, *which proceeds from the fulness of the heart*. It is to no purpose to have our tongue "as the pen of a ready writer," if our hearts be not full. It must come from the boiling or meditation of our hearts, if our profession be good and acceptable.

This is the preface of the song.

Sermon III.[3]

"Thou art fairer than the children of men: grace is poured into thy lips: therefore God hath blessed thee for ever."
Psalm xlv. 2.

I have given you an account of the general design and scope of this psalm already, and spoken something from the title of it, "To the chief Musician," etc.; and opened the 1st verse, and spoken something to that also, which is the preface to the whole psalm.

I shall now speak something to you from the 2nd verse: "Thou art fairer than the children of men: grace is poured into thy lips: therefore God hath blessed thee for ever." You know who it is that is intended in these words, namely, our Lord Jesus Christ, the King, the Messiah; and this is a description of him, which the psalmist gives in prophecy.

There are three parts of the verse: I. A description of *Christ's person*, "Thou art fairer than the children of men." II. An account of his endowments that were bestowed upon him to enable him to his work, "Grace is poured into thy lips." III. God's acceptance and approbation of him in his work, "Therefore God hath blessed thee for ever."

I. Here is a description of Christ's person, "Thou art fairer than the children of men."

You may consider it, 1. Absolutely, that Christ is *fair*. 2. Comparatively, that he is *fairer* than the

---
[3] This sermon was preached at Stadham, June 14, 1674.

children of men.

1. Absolutely: Christ is *fair*. He ascribes beauty to him. There is mention of the beauty of God in Ps. xxvii. 4, "To behold the beauty of the Lord;" — that may concern his worship. But it is directly spoken of God himself, in Zech. ix. 17, "How great is his goodness, and how great is his beauty!" As beauty among men consists in the symmetry of parts, so in God it is the harmony of all the divine perfections. The infinite harmony, agreeableness, suitableness of all divine perfections, I say, is this beauty. Christ is called fair, to denote his glorious perfections.

2. Comparatively: "Thou art *fairer* than the children of men;" that is, (1.) Than all worldly men. There is more excellency, more desirableness in Jesus Christ than in all the men of the world. (2.) More than in all those who were employed in the church, which is peculiarly here intended; more excellent than Moses and Aaron, than any of the kings and prophets of old, who yet were so desirable. Aaron had his garments made for beauty and for glory. But saith he, "Christ is more beautiful, more fair, than any of the children of men."

I told you the design of the psalm was, to speak of the kingdom of Christ, and to set forth the mutual love that is between Christ and his church; but yet, in the first place, he lays down this description of his person as the foundation, "Thou art fairer than the children of men."

I say, 1. Absolutely, Christ is fair; and we may observe from hence, that, in the consideration of Jesus Christ, if we intend any interest in him, and any benefit by him, the first thing we ought to know and consider, is *his person*. So the psalmist here, when he had designed the description of his kingdom and benefits, begins with his person. And if we know not the person of Christ we have no interest in him. The apostle, in Phil.

iii. 10, shows what our design should be, "That I may know him, and the power of his resurrection, and the fellowship of his sufferings," etc. First "know him," says he, before he speaks of the benefits of his mediation; which is consequential to the knowledge of himself. So he tells you, of the subject of his preaching, 1 Cor. ii. 2, "I determined not to know any thing among you, save Jesus Christ, and him crucified;" first Christ, and then him crucified; first his person, and then his mediation.

The reasons are,

(1.) Because Jesus Christ will be loved and preferred above all *for his own sake*. He tells his disciples, Matt. x. 37, "He that loveth father or mother more than me, is not worthy of me." If we intend to have any benefit by him, he must be valued above all for his own sake, or for the sake of what he is in himself. He puts it as a mark upon them that followed him, "Because of the loaves," John vi. 26. And if, without the knowledge of Christ, without a due consideration of his person, we think to follow him only for his benefits, for the advantage which we hope to have by him (which is to follow him for the loaves), we shall be found strangers to him, when we think we are in a better state and condition.

(2.) Without this, no man can secure his love and faith *from being selfish*, or from beginning and ending in self. For if we regard only those things whereof we have advantage, so that we may have our sin pardoned, our iniquities done away, and our souls saved, we would not care whether there were a Christ to trust in or no. But as this tends not to the glory of God, so neither will it tend to the advantage of our own souls. So that if we intend any interest in Christ, we must begin with his person, and the knowledge of it: "Thou art fairer than the children of men."

The use of this point is,

First, To show *how few real Christians* there be in the world, seeing there are so few that have an acquaintance with, and a love unto, the person of Christ. Some deny him. We have a generation among ourselves that pretend to be Christians (I mean the Quakers), who deny the person of Christ, leave him neither the perfection of the Deity, nor humanity, nor the union of his natures; and have framed to themselves a religion without Christ, a carcase without a soul or life to quicken it, or enable it to be of any use. And there are others that evidence how little it is they value Christ. 1 Cor. ii. 8, "Had they known him, they would not have crucified the Lord of glory." Do ye think, if men knew Christ, whatsoever they pretend, they would so despise his ways, his ordinances, his worship? prefer their own inventions and imaginations before them, and prosecute and persecute all that truly fear him, according to the power of their hand? Had they known him, they would not have done so. And the greatest part are perfectly sottish, brutishly ignorant concerning the person of Christ: yea, many to whom he hath been preached, it is to them like the wind, they hear a sound, but know not whence it comes, or what it means; perhaps they never had one serious thought in all their lives what Christ is, or who he is? wherein his excellencies do consist, or what they expect from him. O how few labour to have a familiar intercourse with this Saviour! How few say to wisdom, "Thou art my sister, and call understanding their kinswoman," as in Prov. vii. 4, speaking of Christ, who is the wisdom of God. They that know Christ, will make him as near and familiar to their souls as they can.

Secondly. This shows what great cause *they* have to rejoice, unto whom God hath revealed Christ. Matt. xvi. 13, etc., "Whom do men say I am?" saith Christ to his disciples. "And they said, Some say thou art John the baptist; some, Elias; and others, Jeremias, or one of the prophets. He saith unto them, But whom say ye that I am? And Simon Peter answered and said, Thou art the Christ, the Son of the living God. And Jesus answered and said unto him, Blessed art thou, Simon Bar-jona: for flesh and blood hath not revealed it unto thee, but my Father which is in heaven." The world has very dark notions concerning Christ, like the blind man, that saw men like trees walking: but as for those who have the knowledge of Christ, they are blessed; "for flesh and blood hath not revealed it." It is the greatest spiritual revelation, and the greatest evidence that we have received any spiritual revelation from God, when we know the person of Christ. Let us be thankful for any revelation God hath made of Christ unto our souls; that we behold his person, and know him; that he is not a stranger unto us, but that our souls have some holy acquaintance with him.

And if God hath thus revealed Christ unto us, let us be manifesting to all the world that we are Christ's, when others are ashamed of him. How? By our prizing, valuing, preferring him above all other things; above the world, and all the satisfactions and enjoyments of the world; above its ways, pleasures, converse: we have better satisfaction, better acquaintance to converse with and retire unto.

2. Observe from the words, that, in the knowledge of Christ, what we should chiefly consider are the things wherein he is fairer than the children of men, wherein he is more excellent, and to be preferred above all other persons and things whatsoever.

Now, wherein is Christ fairer than the children of men?

I answer, In three things: (1.) In the dignity of

his person; (2.) In the excellency of his work; and, (3.) In the power and heavenliness of his doctrine. Many other instances may be given, but things may be gathered to these three heads; whereby we may make answer unto the question, that is tacitly asked of us by nominal professors in the world, which was asked of the spouse by the daughters of Jerusalem, Cant. v. 9, "What is thy beloved more than another beloved?" — "What is there in Christ more than in other persons and things, that there is such a stir made about him?" I say, "He is fairer than the children of men."

(1.) In *the dignity of his person*. He is a more excellent person. Wherein consists the excellency of Christ's person? Truly, not at all in the outward appearance of his human nature, especially while here in the world. It is the foundation of all devotion among some, the making of glorious pictures of Christ; by which means to represent him fine and glorious. But what doth he speak of himself in Ps. xxii. 6? "I am a worm, and no man." He was brought to that low condition that he was of no esteem, of no reputation. But if we could have had a sight of him, how comely would he have been! Why, "he had neither form nor comeliness," in his outward appearance, "that when we should see him we should desire him," Isa. liii. 2; wherein, then, consists the dignity of his person? In two things:

[1.] In the glory of his divine nature. [2.] In the immeasurable fulness of his human nature with grace: [1.] In his *divine glory*. Phil. ii. 6, "Who being in the form of God, thought it not robbery to be equal with God." Here is his glory. Also in John i. 14, "We beheld his glory." Wherein consists that glory? "The glory of the only begotten of the Father."

If you ask us, "What is our beloved more than another beloved?" — "What is there in Christ, that our souls are sick of love for him, breathe and pant after the enjoyment of him, and that continually?" It is because we have seen his glory who is God blessed for ever.

[2.] It consists in the immeasurable, unspeakable *fulness of grace* that was given to his human nature. It is what I have as much thought of as any one thing, concerning the immeasurable fulness of grace which is in the human nature of Christ. So saith the apostle, John iii. 34, "God gave not the Spirit by measure unto him." How by measure? "To every one of us is given grace according to the measure of the gift of Christ," Eph. iv. 7. We have every one of us *a measure*; but it is given to him without a measure. There is an immeasurable fulness of grace in the human nature of Christ, which we are partakers of; "for of his fulness we all receive, and grace for grace." It is an infinity in the divine nature, transferred into the human nature of Christ, and through him communicated unto our souls. From the eternal fountain of the divine nature, through the human nature of Christ, which hath an immeasurable fulness, as the head of the church, it is, I say, transfused to all his members. In this he is "fairer than the children of men."

(2.) He is so in *the excellency of his work*. The work that Christ did was such as none ever did or could do, but only he himself. It is true, "The law was given by Moses," but "grace and truth came by Jesus Christ," John i. 17. Could not the law give grace, and do this business, so as to bring in an everlasting righteousness, pardon sin, save the soul, make us accepted with God? No; Rom. viii. 3, "What the law could not do, that God, sending his Son in the likeness of sinful flesh, did." But there were sacrifices of the law; when men had sinned, they could make atonement. No; "Sacrifice and burnt-offerings thou wouldest not. Then said I, Lo, I come to do thy will," Ps. xl. 7. But would there not be righteousness, if men observe the law, and follow after it? Alas! they could not obtain it; Rom. x. 3, 4, "For Christ is the end of the law for righteousness to every one that believeth." So that neither the deeds of the law, nor the sacrifices of the law, nor the righteousness of the law, will do. "The redemption of our souls is precious," and would have ceased for ever, if Christ had not been found to undertake this work. When there was but a book to be opened of revelations for the church, none was found worthy to open it, until Christ prevailed, Rev. v. 2, etc. If there could be no new revelations made but only by Christ, much less could any in heaven or earth redeem the souls of men from death and hell, bring them into favour with God, and work out eternal redemption for them.

(3.) He is more excellent than all the sons of men, *in the revelation he has made of the will of God*. Christ has made such a revelation of the will, love, and grace of God, as none of the children of men ever saw before.

These are the things we ought to consider in Christ, as he is fairer than the children of men, in the dignity of his person, in the excellency of his work, and in the glory of his revelation.

You will say, "*Why* should we consider Christ in these his incomparable excellencies?" I answer,

[1.] *That our hearts be not taken away* nor engrossed by the children of men, and what belongs unto them, their glory, their honours, their lusts, their pleasures, their righteousness. If we would not have our hearts allured and drawn off with them, the way is, to exercise our faith upon the incomparable excellencies of the Lord Jesus Christ. Can the world be to us an all-sufficient God, and a great reward? Can the world pardon our sins, save our souls, deliver us from wrath to come, reveal to us the mystery of truth from the bosom of the Father? Can it make known the mind of God? communicate grace and love to us? If it cannot, then let us dwell in our thoughts on *him* who is fairer than the children of men.

[2.] The consideration of these excellencies in Christ is exceedingly *suited to increase faith and love in us*. They are the proper objects in Christ of these graces. What is it we believe and love? Do not we believe in Christ as the Son of God, as God-man in one person? do not we love him as he is so? do not we believe he hath made atonement for us? and do not we believe and love the excellency of his work? Then the exercise of our thoughts upon these things is the way to increase faith and love in us. And the great reason why we are so weak in our faith, and so cold in our love, is, because we exercise our souls no more to immediate, direct thoughts upon Christ and his excellencies. We live by *reflex* considerations upon the benefits of Christ; but if we could exercise our souls more *directly* in daily thoughts of Christ in faith and love, we should increase more in these graces, and be more transformed into his likeness. "Beholding as in a glass the glory of the Lord, we are changed into the same image," etc., 2 Cor. iii. 18. It is not such a cheap thing to be a Christian as most imagine. What wandering thoughts have the generality of Christians about Christ, and never once examine into their thoughts whether they have any spiritual acquaintance with him or no!

II. The second thing to consider in the words is, *the endowment of Christ, in his human nature*, for the discharge of this great office and work, which is here ascribed unto him in this psalm, set forth by grace being poured into his lips.

And there are three things that may be observed: 1. The nature of this endowment; and that is, *grace*. 2. The manner of its communication, and that is, *poured*; it is not dropped, but poured. 3. The seat of it, being communicated; grace is poured into *his lips*.

1. The nature of this endowment; it is *grace*.

Grace in Scripture is taken two ways: (1.) For *inherent* grace and holiness, or the graces of the Spirit. Things that are bestowed upon men, and wrought in them, they are called grace, the same as the principle of spiritual life. (2.) Grace is taken *externally* for favour and love. "Ye are saved by grace;" that is, by the free favour of God.

It is here taken in the first sense, for the internal principle of grace and holiness. This was poured into the lips of Christ. Grace in the second sense is also mentioned in the last clause of the verse, "Therefore God hath blessed thee for ever."

And we may observe, in reference to the seat of it, that it hath particular respect unto the prophetical office of Christ, whereby he discharged his duty in the revelation of the will of God. Christ did manifest and evidence grace in all he did and said in this world, as the lips are the way of manifesting the mind.

It is the first of these things I shall chiefly discourse on, namely, the endowment that renders the human nature of Christ so exceedingly desirable and glorious, is *grace*.

That which rendered Christ so beautiful, so desirable, and glorious, was not secular wisdom, though there was in him the greatest fulness of all wisdom; it was not the pomp, the greatness, the glory of the world, outward ornaments, or any thing that men esteem: no, it was that which men hate and persecute that rendered Christ so beautiful and glorious. God did not endow Christ with riches; no, he was poor, so poor that he had not where to lay his head: nor with bodily appearance; for he was a worm, and no man. But saith God, "I will render him glorious." How? He shall be full of grace. "We beheld his glory, the glory as of the only begotten of the Father." We saw it, say they; the world saw nothing but a poor man, whom they despised; but *we* saw his glory. And what was that glory? "He was full of grace," John i. 14. Even the glory of Jesus Christ consists in grace.

And why doth this glory of Christ consist in grace? For these three ends:

(1.) Because in this internal grace consists *the reparation of the image of God.* All the glory that God thought meet to communicate to his creature man (and it was unspeakable, and all he designed him for), was to make him in his own image and likeness. This was the glory God intended; every thing else doth but follow it. Now, we left this image, and became as like the devil as if we had been begotten by him. John viii. 44, We are the children of the devil, he is our father; we are a "generation of vipers," the seed of the serpent by nature. But it is grace that doth repair and renew this image of God. It is grace that makes a representation of God unto us; and therefore doth Christ's glory consist in grace. The apostle tells us so, 2 Cor. iv. 6, "We behold the glory of God in the face of Jesus Christ." How is that? Why, in that abounding grace that was in Christ there is made such a representation of God, that there we may see his likeness. It is the human nature of Christ that makes the great representation of God, because he hath all that which is the image and likeness of God — namely, grace in the fulness of it — in him.

(2.) This grace is the glory of Christ, because it is that *which inclines the heart of Jesus Christ* unto all that goodness and kindness that he hath showed unto us. Whence was it that Jesus Christ loved us so as to lay down his life for us? whence does he continue to have compassion on us, even when we were ignorant, and wandered out of the way? It is from that abounding, unspeakable, heavenly love that was in his heart and soul, that inclined him to it. The more grace we have, the more we have of love, compassion, and delight in doing the will of God. But there was that *abundance in Christ* that inclined him to do all this good for us, to live, to die, to intercede for us. This makes Christ very beautiful and glorious to the eye of faith.

(3.) It is the glory of Christ, as he is the great *example* and pattern, whereunto we ought to labour after a conformity. When we had lost all, and wandered up and down, it was not enough that we should have a rule set us, but we must, moreover, have a pattern to follow; we must be like unto Christ. And there is an unconquerable desire implanted in the heart of every believer in the world to be like unto Jesus Christ; because God hath, in the way of an ordinance, appointed him to be our pattern. And we are but trifling Christians, and a dishonour to our profession, if we make not this the design of our souls continually, that we may be in the world as Christ was, that the same mind may be in us that was in him, Phil. ii. 5; the same meekness, humility, self-denial, faith, love, patience, that was in him.

To close in a way of use; if this internal grace and holiness was that wherein Christ was fairer than the children of men, because grace was poured into his lips; then,

1. Let us learn to *esteem* it above all other things. That which rendered Christ beautiful, will render us so: not in the eyes of the world; no, it did not render Christ so to the world; the more he abounded in grace, the more they despised him; but it renders us beautiful *in the sight of God* and all the holy angels, and in the judgment of all be-

lievers upon earth. If we be but like unto Christ in any measure, it will render us fair, beautiful, desirable in the eyes of all that have eyes to see and hearts to discern it.

2. Let us not value so much the lustre, the splendour, and glory that earthly men have in earthly things, in their riches, power, honour, and the like. How apt are we to fret ourselves sometimes at the thoughts of these things; and think they have a peculiar happiness, that they are so great and glorious as they appear and make a show of! But God knows there is nothing in them but what is the object of his contempt, and of all the saints and angels, and will be so to all eternity.

Sermon IV.[4]

*"Gird thy sword upon thy thigh, O most Mighty, with
thy glory and thy majesty."*
Psalm xlv. 3.

In the 2nd verse we have a description of the person of Christ, and of the ground of God's blessing and accepting of him in his work, the psalm having a double design; first, To show the glory of Christ in his kingly office; secondly, To show the mutual love that is between Christ and his church.

This 3rd verse sets forth his entering upon the first part of his work, and is spoken by the way of encouragement unto Christ, in the name of God the Father, to undertake his office, and to go through with it. "Gird thy sword," saith he, "upon thy thigh, O most Mighty, with thy glory and thy majesty."

There are three things in the words: I. The *work* that is proposed unto Jesus Christ, or rather his *preparation* for his work: "Gird thy sword upon thy thigh." II. The *manner how* he should go through this work: "With thy glory and thy majesty." And (that which I shall particularly enlarge on) III. The *appellation* that is here given to Christ; which is, "Most Mighty." He is most mighty in the execution of his office which he is exalted unto:

I. We have Christ's preparation for his work: "Gird thy sword on thy thigh." Consider two things: 1. What is the *sword* of Christ. 2. What is

---
[4] This sermon was preached at Stadham, June 21, 1674.

meant by *girding* this sword upon his thigh.

1. The sword of Christ is the word of God; so it is called, "The sword of the Spirit, which is the word of God," Eph. vi. 17. The Spirit being the great immediate agent whereby Christ administers his kingdom, that which is the sword of the Spirit is the sword of Christ: and therefore, where Christ is described in his kingdom, it is said that "he hath a sword proceeding out of his mouth," Rev. i. 16; which, in another place, is called "The rod of his mouth," Isa. xi. 4. It is the word of God, the great instrument of Christ in managing of his kingdom, that is called here his sword.

2. Concerning this it is said, "Gird thy sword upon thy thigh." The girding of the sword upon the thigh, is the putting of it into readiness for use. When David was going up against Nabal, he said unto his men, 1 Sam. xxv. 13, "Gird ye on every man his sword." Wherefore Christ's girding his sword upon his thigh, is the disposing of the word into the ordinances of the gospel, where it may be ready for use. It hath respect unto the time when he ascended on high, and sent forth his word for the setting up of his kingdom. Then he put his word in readiness to effect the great designs of his love and grace, when "he gave some apostles, and some prophets, and some evangelists, and some pastors and teachers," Eph. iv. 11. He furnished men with gifts and abilities to dispense this word unto the ends of his kingdom.

II. The *manner* of going through his work is, "With thy glory and thy majesty." The glory and majesty of Christ are his power and authority. And so it is prophesied of, as an encouragement unto the Lord Christ, that he should clothe his word with power and authority for the ends of setting up his kingdom, the edification of his church and the preservation of it in the world.

These things I speak in a general way; I shall

now more particularly address myself,

III. To the appellation that is here given unto Christ, "O most Mighty, גבור, from גבר, one that prevails in every thing he takes in hand.

Observe from hence, that the Lord Jesus Christ, as king of the church, is endowed with a mighty power for the accomplishing of all the designs and ends of this rule and kingdom. It is said of him, Ps. lxxxix. 19, God hath "laid help upon one that is mighty." It is spoken there primarily of David, "I have found David my servant." But what could poor David do? one taken from the sheepfold. It was not a laying help, therefore, upon David that was mighty, absolutely speaking; but a putting strength into him. But David was a type of Christ; and to him must the passage be referred; he is the mighty One. Also Isaiah, Isa. lxiii. 1, describing of Christ in his kingdom, saith, "It is 'I that speak in righteousness, mighty to save.'" And again, in Ps. xxiv. 7, etc., there is a description of his ascension into heaven; the gates and everlasting doors being lifted up, that he, the King of glory, may enter in. The question being asked, "Who is this King of glory?" saith he, "The Lord, strong and mighty." It is a property everywhere ascribed unto Jesus Christ, that he is mighty.

Here we may inquire, 1. *Whence* Christ is thus mighty for the execution of his kingly office? and, 2. *To what ends* he doth put forth this might and power?

1. *Whence* is Christ thus mighty? Christ is mighty upon two accounts:

(1.) From the *omnipotent power* of his divine nature; which is the principle of his mighty operations in the union of his person. So the prophet declares, Isa. ix. 6, "Unto us a child is born, unto us a son is given." And how shall he be called? "Wonderful, Counsellor, The mighty God;" —

"This child that is born unto us, this son that is given unto us, his name shall be (that is, he really is), The mighty God." Why so? Because of the union of the divine nature with the human in the same person; whereby the same person becomes a child born, and also the mighty God.

(2.) He is mighty, from the *authority* and power that was *communicated* and given unto him *by the Father*, as mediator, for the accomplishing of his whole work. Two things concur to make one legally mighty to proper ends; first, strength and power; secondly, authority. Where there is strength and power and no authority, it is force; and where there is authority, but no strength or power, that authority will be void. Christ had strength and power as the mighty God; and he hath authority too, as all power is communicated to him by God the Father; as may be seen in Matt. xxviii. 18; Eph. i. 20-22, and many other places.

But it will be objected, "If Christ be the mighty God *by nature*, how comes it to pass that he should have power and authority *given unto him*? God hath given unto him might and dominion, far above all principalities," etc.

I answer, Christ, as his power is given to him, is considered not absolutely as God, nor absolutely as man; but as *God-man*, Mediator, one that mediates between God and man: and so his power to erect his kingdom is given him of his Father.

2. The second inquiry is, *Unto what ends* doth the Lord Jesus put forth this mighty power wherewith he is endowed? I answer, To these five ends: (1.) Unto the erecting of his kingdom or church in the world; (2.) To the preservation of it; (3.) To the subduing of his enemies; (4.) To the raising of the dead; (5.) In the judging of all flesh, and distributing of eternal rewards and punishments: all which are acts of mighty power.

(1.) Jesus Christ puts forth this mighty power

in *erecting and building of his church*. In Matt. xvi. 18, our Lord saith, "I will build my church;" and the apostle, in Heb. iii. 3, 4, shows that it was *an act of divine power* to build this church of God: "He that built all things is God." No one could build a church in all ages, but God himself. And if we were able to take a view how Jesus Christ first built his church in the world, we should learn not to distrust his power in any thing he had afterward to do. There was a combination of hell and of all the power of the world, against the interest of Christ and the gospel. The concurring suffrage of mankind, wise and unwise, learned and unlearned, Jew and Greek, influenced by their interest, by all that was dear unto them, set themselves in a combination against Christ's building of his kingdom. He employed against all this force a *few poor men*, unlearned, unskillful; and gives into their hands only the sword of the Spirit, the word of God; furnishes them only with gifts and abilities for the dispensing of the word: which was "his girding of his sword upon his thigh." He set these poor men to work; and clothing them with his glory and majesty, they make havoc in the devil's kingdom, and destroy it by degrees, until they root it out of the earth. It was, then, an act of mighty power in Christ, to build his kingdom and church.

(2.) Christ puts forth this mighty power *in the preserving of his church*, being so founded and built on him. It is that which he expresses, Isa. xxvii. 3, "I the Lord do keep it; I will water it every moment: lest any hurt it, I will keep it night and day."

The church being built, is not able to stand of itself; for unto the end of time the gates of hell and the power of the world shall be engaged against it. But saith he, I will keep it, "and the gates of hell shall not prevail against it." There is a carnal church in the world, or a worldly church; and how is *that* kept? By force, laws and power of men who have wrapt up their secular interest in the preserving of it; and they will fight for their kingdom. On the contrary, the Lord Jesus Christ hath a *spiritual church*, of them that believe in him. They also are preserved; and by what means? By *a secret emanation* of mighty power from Jesus Christ. There hath not been any age in the world since the ascension of Christ, but there hath been an emanation, or putting forth of this mighty power of Christ in preserving of this church. He preserved a people under the whole apostasy of Antichrist. Had there been none left on the earth to fear him, and believe in him, all the promises of God to him had come to an end. But he did secretly, by his mighty power, preserve a people to himself in the midst of all the defection of Antichrist. And he doth so at this day, in the midst of the new defection made to Antichrist: for, in former days, the world fell off to Antichrist by superstition and idolatry; they are now falling off to him by profaneness and atheism: yet Jesus Christ, by his mighty power under both, or by a secret exertion of his power, preserves his church through all, and carries them as safe through the *new* opposition as he did through the *old*.

(3.) He puts forth his power for the *subduing* and conquering of his and his church's *enemies*.

What enemies has Christ? what enemies has the church? As many as there are devils in hell, and men and women in the world that are of the seed of the serpent. But I may reduce all the enmity to the interest of Christ upon earth to these four heads: [1.] Satan; [2.] The world; [3.] Sin; [4.] Death. Christ is most mighty in conquering all these enemies:

[1.] He puts forth his mighty power in conquering of *Satan*. This was the first word that was spoken of him in the world, in Gen. iii. 15, "I will put enmity between thee and the woman, and between thy seed and her seed: it shall bruise thy head, and thou shalt bruise his heel." The first discovery God made to his creatures concerning the incarnation of his Son was in this, that he would destroy Satan; and so the Holy Ghost tells us he hath done, Col. ii. 15, "He spoiled principalities and powers, and made a show of them openly, triumphing over them in his cross." These words, "He spoiled principalities and powers," are an exposition of the former promise in Genesis, that "the seed of the woman" (Jesus Christ) "should bruise the serpent's head." How should he do it? Why, in spoiling principalities and powers, and triumphing over them openly in his cross. So he saith, in Heb. ii. 14, "That through death he might destroy him that had the power of death, that is, the devil." He did not destroy him as to his *being*, but as to his *power* and authority. Hence, first, the devil hath a limited power only remaining, such as shall never prejudice the eternal interest of the church; and, secondly, He is reserved unto eternal destruction by this mighty power of Christ.

[2.] The second enemy of Christ is the *world*; and that may be considered either in the men of it or in the power of it:

In *the men* of it. The Lord Christ puts forth his mighty power to deal with and subdue all the men of the world that rise up in opposition against him. Whatever success they may seem to have, they are all made his footstool: "Thou shalt break them with a rod of iron; thou shalt dash them in pieces like a potter's vessel," Ps. ii. 9. And you have him twice or thrice described in the Revelation as going forth in his mighty power for the subduing of all his adversaries. See Rev. xix. 11–21.

And this *must* be; for he shall subdue all the

authority in the world, not only the *persons* of men, but all the *power* and all the authority which is set up against him, or exercised against his interest. 1 Cor. xv. 24, 25, "When he shall have put down all rule and all authority and power. For he must reign, till he hath put all enemies under his feet." There is a suspension of the issue of all things until Christ hath thus put down all that opposeth him and his interest. But there is an expectation in heaven, and in earth, in the whole creation: all are waiting, as if one single person, for the putting forth this mighty power of Christ for the subduing of all unto him; for the end will not be till then. Whatever we endure, we must be contented with it; whatsoever we suffer, the end must not be till all his enemies be made his footstool, and there be nothing to stand up against him who is most mighty.

[3.] *Sin* in his people is another *enemy of Christ*. Sin, as it is in men by nature, is that which gives life and efficacy to all the enmity that is acted against him; and, as it remains even in believers themselves, it doth act a great enmity against Christ. How come we, then, to be freed from it? how comes it to be subdued? The apostle, in Rom. vii., gives an account of the great contest and conflict that believers have with the remainder of sin in them, that makes them cry out for deliverance from it, verses 24, 25. It is a sudden breaking forth of the apostle there, when he was describing the law of sin; for he cries out, "O wretched man that I am! who shall deliver me?" etc. But he as suddenly takes up, "I thank God, through Jesus Christ our Lord;" — "Through the power of Christ this enemy, sin, shall be subdued." Therefore, chap. vi. 14, it is said, "Sin shall not have dominion over you: for ye are not under the law, but under grace;" — "If you come under grace, or under the rule of Christ, sin shall not have dominion over you." What is the reason of it? where is the consequence of the argument? Because sin is one great enemy of Christ, and he will certainly conquer it.

[4.] *Death* is another enemy. It is the last enemy, 1 Cor. xv. 25, 26, "He must reign, till he hath put all enemies under his feet. The last enemy that shall be destroyed is death." And, in verse 54, he tell us that "death is swallowed up in victory;" a conquest is obtained over it. It is the last enemy, because, until the consummation of all things, we shall be subject to its power; but *that* shall also come under the feet of Christ, when we shall die no more.

This is the third end wherefore Christ puts forth this mighty or exceeding greatness of his power, namely, for the subduing of his enemies.

(4.) The fourth end for which Christ puts forth the greatness of his power is, for the *raising up all his church from the dead*, Phil. iii. 20, 21, "Our conversation is in heaven; from whence also we look for the Saviour, the Lord Jesus Christ: who shall change our vile body, that it may be fashioned like unto his glorious body, according to the working whereby he is able even to subdue all things unto himself." The mighty power of Christ reaches thus far, that the dead shall be raised thereby. Yes, our vile body shall, the body of our humiliation; that is, the body as it is fallen into corruption, into a vile estate, though it come to worms and dust, yet he shall revive it by the exceeding greatness of his power. He shall raise the bodies of his people. The privilege of believers in that day will be, that they shall be first raised, and they shall be peculiarly raised by the power of Christ as mediator. Their bodies shall be raised in conformity to his glorious body, when others shall be raised after them by the mere divine power of Christ, and raised with all their own vileness upon them.

(5.) And lastly, to mention no more; the

mighty power of Christ is put forth in *judging of all the world*, and distributing to them rewards of bliss or woe that shall abide to all eternity, Matt. xxv. 31–46.

Thus you see why the Holy Ghost, by the psalmist, calls Christ here the Mighty One, one that will mightily prevail in every thing. It is because of his divine power, he is the mighty God. Because of his mediatorial authority there is committed unto him all power in heaven and in earth. He doth put forth this power for the erecting of his church, for its preservation, for the subduing of his enemies, in the raising of the dead, and distributing rewards and punishments.

Printed in Great Britain
by Amazon